Do You Even Know Who You Are?

Isaac Malachi Peters

BookLeaf Publishing

Presentation by *BookLeaf Publishing*

Web: www.bookleafpub.com

E-mail: info@bookleafpub.com

ISBN: 9789357442169

First edition 2023

ACKNOWLEDGEMENT

First and foremost, I give thanks to God; The source from whom all my gifts and abilities flow.

To the woman I love, my inspiration and motivation for several pieces contained in this book I thank you for your unwavering support and belief, without you this wouldn't be possible.

My family and friends, your encouragement has been invaluable, any success I achieve is a testament to the relationships we have fostered and I'm truly grateful for each and every one of you.

PREFACE

To some, the relatability of the poems contained in this book will reinforce the knowledge that you are not alone in your experiences and to others, this poem will expose you to an alternative worldview.

Regardless, the aim is to make you feel something.

Enjoy.

Unapologetically Me

I've often found myself trying to be like water...
You know,
A conformist.
Imagining myself to be fluid but in reality
breaking my back and twisting my tongue to fit
into the mold of society.
I thought being a chameleon meant that I was
adaptable,
A man of many masks.
My face, interchangeable with the time and
place in which I find myself.
Ironic that phrase...
"Find myself"
What does that even mean?
Who am I really?
Where would I go to find myself when the "me"
I seek is dependent on the "me" you wish to see.
I heard a saying once that your true self is who
you are when no one is looking
I guess the real question is...
Do I even truly know who that is?

Puberty

This is a strange time
And by that I mean I feel like a stranger in the
body I once called mine
There's growth in places and psychological
changes that frankly I'm not sure if I like
Hormones are raging like a horse in heat
And the desires I have expressed…
I'm not sure I should repeat.
That being said,
I like the height and the depth in my tone
I also love the fact that everyone seems to have
noticed the new hairs I've grown
But if I'm being honest
This is new territory
So I'm navigating this unfamiliar frame
carefully.
Trying not to make too many adjustments so as
not to deviate too far from the original design
But in the event that I do...
I just hope that in my search for myself I like
what I find.

Answer

Growing up I was a very curious kid
I've always had questions
The world is a huge conglomerate of
information
There are certain things I have come to learn
And others I never will

There are known knowns
There are known unknowns
And even still
There are unknown unknowns
But you...
You fall into the last category

I didn't know I needed you till you were here
The missing piece to my jigsaw puzzle
You thought you were awkwardly shaped till we
combined and you made me whole
I've always had questions
But you...
You are my answer

Cover

Okay so let's get one thing straight
I may speak street vernacular
But don't ever mistake that to mean
That I don't be intelligent
Or that man is dumb
My medium of communication is meticulous in
meaning
I've got metaphors mighty enough to weigh
heavily on your mind
And remind you that books are meant to be read
And covers are not to be used as a measure of
judgment
Maybe next time, instead of imposing your
ignorance on me
Try cracking open my cover with a salutation,
Flip through my pages with casual conversation
And at-least attempt to suppress your
amazement at my intelligence.
You might just learn something.

Renaissance

On some days I wake up more perplexed than
focussed
My hindsight far surpassing my foresight
Looking backwards has me lacking the
momentum I need to press forward towards the
man I intend to be

I feel like my life has gone through various
stages
As I've progressed through various phases
I've realized that maturity and development
aren't dependent on ages
It's the changes that we make that take us places

And I've got places I want to go
I wasn't always this way
My thought processes could have been described
as archaic
Living to satisfy my present need
I was living life myopically
Too short-sighted to see that the me I seek
resides beyond my present reality

But as is the only guarantee in this life
I changed
Call it my renaissance period

I made efforts each day to die as my head hit the
pillow and each morning as the sun rose so
would I
Resurrected a new creation
Yesterday's mistakes dead and buried
Fresh zeal coursing through my veins
You might call it strange
I call it progress

This is what it takes
You have to sacrifice sleep in order to live your
dreams
And personally
I just want to be better than the man I was
yesterday
As long as I can do that
I'll be happy

Cry

I saw him bleed transparent fluid from his eyes
I stood utterly confused
He was doing exactly what he'd always told me
not to
What strange hypocrisy is this?

He's crumbling before my very eyes
The entirety of his six foot frame trembling
What do I do here?
Do I comfort him?

I look down at my clenched fist
My immediate reaction to punch him
Tell him to get it together
Like he told me all those times
It's like I'm emotionally dyslexic
Incapable of translating his feelings

Instead, I let him know I see him
I go against everything within me
I lift his head and tell him it's okay
Let it all out
This is what being a man is all about

Allow yourself to feel
Don't deny the pain is real
Embrace it,
Look at it in its face
And then let it go
Just let it all go

I see as the weight of shame falls from his frame
He stands now
Erect
Eyes still leaking but renewed in the knowledge
he hasn't lost anything

He is still my father
And I love him.

Innocence

I see beauty in your eyes
I see beauty in your disguise
I see beauty in the lies,
You told in futile attempts to mask your soul in
bravado
But you left the backdoor open and your truth
stumbled out
A phenomenally fragile image of a child
With nothing but love and hope in her eyes
The picture of innocence
Bounding towards me
With each step getting more hopeful
Less than a meter between us now and she's
beaming with happiness
I kneel,
Arms outstretched like branches of an oak tree
She leaps into my arms but is snatched mid-air
And dragged back into the abyss of your
despair...
At least I got to see her.

Battle of The Day

You open your eyes,
and for a fleeting moment you're at peace with
the world,
Flashes of the dream your alarm clock had just
resuscitated you from; linger in your mind,
bringing a smile to your lips
But before you can revel in the memory
You notice a slight tremor beneath your feet,
the rumbling sound of their footsteps is heard
almost instantly in the distance,
The army of innumerable thoughts rushing to
attack your self-esteem.
Frantically your fingers search your sheets to
find the device from which you draw strength.
It's Fully charged,
time for you to get plugged in
You instinctively tap the Instagram icon and 52
DM's await your attention,
calling cards you might say
Each a suggestion of intentions to shower you
with affection
But twice you've given your heart to jokers and
you have vowed to never allow yourself to get
played again.

It took more than a few spades to dig up the
courage to open up to anyone new.
You remind yourself that you're a queen and that
pressure makes diamonds
You take solace in the thought that your king
still awaits
Not in dive bars or clubs
But in nice cars or decks of ships you can cruise
on.
Your father always said you were his rose
And that's why he sowed all he had in the fertile
soil of your upbringing
Tenderly untying the tangles in your hair
Watering you daily with his love and adoration
Teaching you that you could do and become
anything you wanted
If you could conceive it and believe it then it
was only a matter of time before you achieved it
In hopes that these seeds would penetrate deep
and eventually cultivate a plantation of
productivity in your spirit.
Or at least build a wall of confidence.
Solid enough to keep out the noise of
discouragement that so frequently plagues your
mind.
The tremor feels more like an earthquake now as
they inch closer and the realization that you
cannot remain here in this bed becomes more
and more undeniable.

You must face the world again today.
Still licking the wounds from yesterday's battle,
You gird yourself with the words of affirmation
He taught you, kiss the picture of you and him
on your dresser and venture out to war.
Today is a new day.

What Are We?

Nothing good comes after this question
It's less of a question and more of an accusation
An accusation as to whether this is a fling or
something real
Forcing you to reveal how you really feel
There's no right answer.
You're left with a choice
Whether to push on towards the eventuality of
the dreaded 'relationship'
Or simply let go
And cast your line in another direction
As they say
There are plenty of fish in the sea.

But you know what you see in her.
The undeniable truth is that
While you were playing mind games
You took your eye off the ball
Lost control and took a fall
Into the abyss that many refer to as
"Feelings"
So before you nonchalantly stroll out of her life
Consider carefully,
Are you walking out of another fling
Or did you just lose your wife?

Situationship

You were so desperate for affection that you
snorted the cocaine line of lust and filled your
lungs with lies believing the high would mirror
what you imagined love would look like
Only to be surprised at the hollowness you felt
inside

They were always themselves
You chose to see what wasn't there
You mistook the red flags for banners of
devotion and dove headfirst into the
situationship
That capsized your dreams of a healthy
relationship
And yet you wonder why you still feel so alone

Writer's Block

As I pick up the pen to write
Or my phone to type
In desperate attempt to search my mind
to find the right rhymes or punchlines
To really bring to life
The poetry boiling beneath the surface,
I often find myself stuck
It's frustrating like a yawn that won't come out
Or like waiting for a girl to get dressed
The relationship between my pen and my mind
is like that of a divorced couple
Sometimes they reminisce and remember when
they were once in sync and from afar, they
appear to flow in harmony
at other times you'd think that they were at
violent odds
Leaving my heart to be the bloody referee
between them
Stuttered speech and forgotten lines are the
symptoms of their brawl
The still-born poems in my soul are the offspring
awaiting Child protective services to take them
to another home.
My mind blames itself and my pen blames her
too.

I stare at this blank page like the bully at
lunchtime
Intimidated like a house of straw facing a
whirlwind
My heart is my hype man
"Just put pen to paper" it says
"What's the worst that could happen?"
Well actually a lot,
I might pen down my deepest darkest secrets
and release my worst fears
Giving life to what was only a thought, now let
loose on the world to wreak havoc.
I might expose to scrutiny the parts of myself
I've fought my entire adult life to protect.
I might ruin the facade of bravado that
epitomizes my self-image.
The writing process is like surgery
It gets ugly and you're never really sure of the
outcome.
It's painful but necessary
It opens you up and excavates your core essence
Leaving you bare but also disturbingly refreshed
Look at what we made.

Friendship

Who would have thought that we'd be friends
That this broken bridge we could ever mend
Why is it that our minds collide
In times and places we seem to find
Through turbulence this friendship grew
Into something more than we ever knew

Destiny

They say that a man is most powerful when in
tune with his purpose
I've also heard that we're all here for a reason
Otherwise we'd all look, sound and act the same
So why do I feel like I can't find my own lane
Like anything I want to achieve has been done
or is unattainable
"Impossible is nothing" Adidas tells me
And Nike instructs that I "Just do it";
So here it is
I'm pouring out my heart on pages and on
screens
Exposing my secrets and vulnerabilities
Because despite what the gnawing voice in my
head says
This is my purpose
I do have something of value to say
My thoughts are of substantial contribution
My existence is a colourful addition to the mural
we like to call life
So I'm laying myself bare for all to see
That I too,
Finally,
Have been able to find...
My destiny.

Hypothetical Phobia

I don't believe in fearing that which I cannot
control
Therefore these are merely unpleasant thoughts I
wish had never wandered across the plane of my
mind.

I fear osmosis
Where I gradually but almost certainly lose my
essence to my surroundings
Where I start to shed my mane
And develop an appetite for grass as my roar is
replaced by bleating and the urge to follow
others rather than charting my own path.
A reality where I trade soaring above clouds for
an earth-bound existence defenseless against
those that seek my demise.

I fear looking into the eyes of those of whose
lives I contributed in creating and not having
anything to offer them.
I fear witnessing my descendants follow a path I
have trailed that leads only to regret.
I fear waking up one morning and rolling over to
see an empty imprint in the bed where my rib
once was

Leaving my heart exposed and vulnerable to damage.

I fear that my tombstone will say nothing more than the fact that I merely existed, consumed oxygen and left not so much as a fleeting footprint on this earth.
But most of all I fear what's next.
When the game is over, I finally stop running and death tags me 'it'
Will I be ready for who and what awaits me?
I don't know.
It is for this reason I fear nothing but trust in Him whose awesome presence dispels fear's very existence.
I am fearless for I am free.

Race

On the starting line of this race or shall I say
marathon,
Tethered to my competition
I anticipate my victory
Those to whom I am shackled are actually meant
to be on my team and not my competition
But do they know this?
Because as we make our ascent up this
treacherous trail
The further I get
The harder they pull to keep me where they are
Whilst concurrently screaming words of
encouragement
I'm confused
Because I firmly believe a win for me is a win
for us but my race seems to be inhibiting me
from reaching first place.

So now what do I do?
Deny my caterpillar phase now that I'm a
butterfly?
I can't help but question why?
What is it about this skin that hates what we
believe we cannot have?

That doesn't know how to save but is quick to
grab what doesn't belong to them.
What is it about me,
That makes me feel like I owe it to my race to be
great
Like it's of some greater significance if I
succeed
I'm only doing this so my kids have food to eat
and a place to sleep
It's really not all that deep
But there's all this imposed pressure
Pressure to belong to this caste,
This ethnic group
This culture
This race
Why can't I just be human?

Police Brutality

Officer I get it
I really do
You obviously feared for your life
That hooded 14-year-old boy probably had a
knife
He could have taken you away from your
children and your wife
I mean what other option did you have
What would a mere taser have done
The melanin in his skin is clearly immune to
electricity
His complexion obviously shows that he doesn't
understand simple instructions like freeze and
don't move
That confused expression on his face didn't fool
you no, not one bit
You can almost see his thought process on his
face
He's about to attack you
So of course at the slightest twinge of a muscle
you scream gun and rain lead
Filling his brown body with iron like he was
anemic
Then of course you cuff his coloured corpse
before he raises from the dead

Because we all know how this kind doesn't
know how to stay down
A slap on the wrist and paid leave is what you
get
While his mother is struggling to breathe as she
grieves
"My son was supposed to bury me" she screams
As she lays to rest the boy she delivered who
never grew into the man she envisioned

Misunderstood

She loves me
Her words are daggers and her tongue is a knife
One that has cut me several times
But I know she loves me
How?
Because this same blade has defended me on
countless occasions
But when you wield a weapon as deadly as this
you're bound to get power drunk.
And that's okay

She loves me
Her rants are well-intentioned
But they fall like bricks upon my confidence
Her advice sometimes sounds like berating
But I know she loves me
How?
Because she also uses these words to uplift me
She sees the me that exists in realms beyond
reality
The me that I can be
It's just when she sees what I am...
It frustrates her
She knows I can be so much more
But that's okay

I know she loves me

Heartbreak

Like a bull in a china shop you home-invaded
my heart
Leaving nothing but debris and destruction in
your wake
I wake up each day wondering if it's my wake
because I'm surrounded by those that love me
but I can't feel anything
Well anything except this massive ache in my
chest where my heart once was.
Because you took that too.
Most of it at least,
I still have a few broken shards I have no idea
how I'll piece together
or if I even want to
because the only thing I'm sure of…
is the fact that all I want is you.
But you seem to elude me like my shadow in a
well-lit room
Someone that was meant to be with me at all
times but is nowhere to be found
Leaving me less than whole
Incomplete.

The name of this poem was going to be
"heartache"
But a quick glance in my chest and you'll find it
was more appropriately titled heartbreak

Glass

We had something great
Something beautiful
Something we could call our own
We had something
But something wasn't what we needed
We needed something definite
We needed a title
A name
A definition
But for what we had there wasn't one that quite
fit
Our love would crack every time we'd ascribe
one to it

The sand we melted and molded into our
masterpiece
Was so beautiful we forgot it was fragile
Beauty does not equal strength
And strength is born from struggle
What if our castle of glass wasn't built to last

What if it was made to be a monument
One that like so many others was there only for
a fleeting moment to inspire others
Our very own city of Atlantis

A place only we can go
Safely tucked away in our memory

At least I like to think that it is
We threw one stone too many in this house of
glass
And shattered it completely
I'm just glad that we were able to break the
ceiling
Even if we don't get to have it all
Maybe someone else will
Maybe

Transition

Loss is a strange thing
The feeling of a vacuum where something once
was
A hollow sensation
Sometimes it comes with a sense of relief
A tumor being torn from healthy flesh
The creation of space to replace what was killing
you

But now what do I fill this vacancy with?
Or better yet…
Who?
I mean there's no way I can go back to you
I'm on a mission to transition from the man you
made me become
Into the one I was created to be

I AM FREE!
Free from the box you craftily crammed my soul
into
Free!
Free from the lies and deceit I bought into
Free!
Free from being forced to drink this cocktail of
bootleg love and God knows what else

You were sick
But rather than allow me nurse you back to
health you cajoled me into drinking the same
poison that ailed you
Just so we'd have something in common
But now that this surgery has unburdened me
There's no way I'm going back

I am free.

The Walk (Salvation)

Rain beats relentlessly against my skin,
I pray it penetrates and cleanses me within,
But I know that nothing can purge this heart of
sin;
Nothing but the blood of Jesus.
I put one foot in front of the other,
the journey of a thousand miles begins with a
step they say,
But imagine walking that thousand miles,
only to realise you went the wrong way.

I can feel the stares and glares of the onlookers
Catching looks of disapproval from pastors and
even the hookers,
But who am I to complain,
Why can't they all be like this rain
That treats us all equally
Not with pity or disdain
But falls on us all the same
whether born into abject poverty..
or into money and fame.
It gets harder to walk
It wasn't always this way.

There used to be a group of us...

Now I'm alone... my chin goes up
Defiance is my only form of defence
Defiance of society and all its pretence
I feel like everyone can see through me
Like their opinions are X Rays on my thoughts
I'm actually scared...
My emotions have me shaking like branches in a
storm
I have tried to ignore this for too long
And I had hoped that like the incessant nagging
of a troubled wife it would eventually ebb and I
would be okay but...
Jesus.
Jesus is the only way right now and I admit it...
Because this is a truth...
and like all other truth it sets me free
The best part though
is that this isn't just A truth...
it's The truth...
I'm scared... of tomorrow,
of other people,
of myself...
The Bible says that He has done all things well...
So I keep walking
Putting one foot in front of the other
Praying I meet you at my destination.